D07753863

A must read for young adults beginning their careers! Dr. Kelly provides readers with strong advice to set themselves up for future success. Covering vital topics such as an Emergency Fund, these important lessons have already been lifesavers.

— 2nd LT Kainoa Ho
US Air Force

Mary Kelly is the military version of Suze Orman ... energetic, enthusiastic and she makes it easy to understand money.

— Jennifer G. Pilcher
Founder & CEO of MilitaryOneClick.com

Common sense isn't common, especially about money. This book shows you how to get your financial life off to a great start!

— Dan Janal
Founder, PR LEADS, LEADS.com
Author of *Internet Marketing Confidential*

Being financial responsible is something everyone should learn early. Having money means having freedom.

— Debbie Taylor
Taylor Made Events and Speakers
www.taylormadeeventsandspeakers.com

I hate personal finance books. Which is why I love THIS book. Mary Kelly does a masterful job in providing "just enough, just in time" advice, insights and recommendations. This book will not only rock your world - it could very well save your life. Buy it. Use it. Do it!"

— David Newman
Author of *Do It! Marketing: 77 Instant-Action Ideas to Boost Sales, Maximize Profits, and Crush Your Competition*
www.DoItMarketing.com

Real solutions for today's personal financial challenges-a great tool for your money management tool box.

— Carmen M. Perez
Author of *Bounce Back Journal*
www.GalPalBounceBackGetaways.com

Productive Leaders

MONEY $MART

How Not to Buy Cat Food
When You Don't Have a Cat

$ $ $ $ $

*The least you need to know to
be prepared, succeed financially,
and live comfortably.*

Mary C. Kelly, PhD

Published by:

Kaimana Publishing
P. O. Box 461350
Denver, CO 80246

www.ProductiveLeaders.com

Printed in the U.S. by www.minibuk.com

ISBN 978-1-935733-15-7

Special Thanks

Several people were helpful with suggestions for this book. They helped me read it for accuracy and provided encouragement and ideas. Specifically, I wish to thank:

Second Lieutenant Kaitlin Glitz, for finding pictures of T-zo Fox, and Second Lieutenant Tom Lerum for giving me permission to use them.

The US Air Force Academy, the US Naval Academy, and Hawaii Pacific University for entrusting me with their cadets, midshipmen, students, and everyone who attended my classes and personal finance seminars.

Eric Reinhold, USNA, 1988 former Midshipmen Financial Advisor, Certified Financial Planner®, and President of Academy Wealth Management.
www.academywealth.com

George Carradini, USNA 1984, Certified Financial Planner®, Managing Partner, Carradini Wealth Management Advisors.

Linda Jacob, Certified Financial Planner®, Wealth Manager for Integrity Bank & Trust.
www.integritybankandtrust.com

$

Table of Contents

Introduction

The impetus for my writing this book
was my students—cadets at the U.S. Air
Force Academy and the U.S. Military
Academy, midshipmen at the U.S.
Naval Academy, and my Hawaii Pacific
University students.

This book is dedicated to all those
who serve others, with my heartfelt
hope that they make good decisions
and lead well.

Proceeds from this book are
donated to:

The Wounded Warrior Project
www.woundedwarriorproject.org

Take Me Home Pet Rescue
www.takemehomepetrescue.com

Together We Can Change The World
www.twcctw.org

$

Goals of This Book

The goal of this book is to give 20- to 30-year-olds a quick reference guide on what they need to know about personal finance.

Money itself does not equate to happiness. However, it is hard to be happy if you are hungry, are financially stressed, or cannot provide for your family.

Money is a tool used to maintain a comfortable lifestyle and then to help others.

This is the book I wish someone had given me when I was 18. And 20. And 25.

In this book you will learn to:

- Develop a saving and spending plan

- Get out of debt and stay out of debt forever

- Manage debt and credit wisely

- Be prepared for financial emergencies

- Be confident about your ability to maintain a quality standard of living throughout your working and retirement years

- Understand why it is so important to start being smart now

- Spend less, save more, and live better

- Never fight about money with the person you love

$

Do You Need This Book?

As an economist, I don't want you to waste money on a book that you don't need. Take this 10-question quiz to determine whether or not this book will be helpful for you.

True   False   I always save at least 10 percent of my pretax income.

True   False   I can explain the difference between a stock and a bond to a 10-year-old child.

True	False	I have a Roth IRA, and I fully funded it for the last three years.
True	False	If I am working, I maximize individual contributions to my company's retirement plan—i.e., 401(k), Thrift Savings Plan (government and military). If I am self-employed, I have a Defined Benefit Plan, SEP, solo 401(k) or SIMPLE IRA.

True False I do not have any student loans.

True False I do not have any debt except for the mortgage on my home.

True False I can afford to pay off (or I paid off) my car.

True False I pay off all of my credit cards every month.

True False I never lose sleep over financial issues.

True False I have a solid understanding of finances. I accept responsibility for my own financial situation, and I do not accept financial help from my parents, friends, or the government.

If you answered "True" to everything on this list, go have a coffee and pat yourself on the back. You are doing great!

If you answered "False" to any of these statements, this book can help you become financially independent, wise, and, ultimately, wealthy.

$

Mary's Money Tips

When teaching economics I start the class with a "Money Tip of the Day." A few favorites are:

1. Spend less than what you make after taxes are deducted. (Don't spend what you don't have.)

2. Pay yourself first. Set up an allotment directly into a savings or retirement account so that you don't miss the money. If you don't see the money and cannot access it, don't spend it.

3. Understand compound interest and the value of saving money early.

4. Prioritize monthly spending, such as the rent or house payment, the car payments, gas, tuition, and food.

5. Buy the car you need and can afford. Having a car that is too expensive for your lifestyle is a burden.

6. Own your own home only if you are going to be in a certain location for three to five years. Otherwise, the taxes, fees, commissions, stress, and hassle of buying and

selling in a shorter amount of time generally make the process unprofitable.

7. Eating out, even if you are going to a drive-through, is a luxury. That includes coffee and soda.

8. If you are short of cash, don't subject yourself to temptation. Only shop at grocery stores. Stay away from malls and online shopping opportunities.

9. Be responsible for your own retirement. Start and fund a Roth Individual Retirement Account if you are eligible.

10. Contribute to employer-sponsored retirement plans, especially if there is any kind of matching available.

Chapter 1

Why Get Smart Now?

I was teaching a personal finance class at a university and had a student who proudly told the class that she was totally ready for retirement at the young age of 34. I was impressed and asked if she would share how she prepared.

"Beanie Babies™!" she exclaimed. "I have been collecting Beanie Babies™ for years, and I think that when I am ready to retire they will be worth a fortune!"

Sadly, she was not kidding.

Beanie Babies are not a retirement plan.

Many people think they are prepared for retirement when they are not. Many working people don't think about retirement because it seems like such a long way off. As of this writing, one-third of Americans have no retirement savings.

But retirement is only part of the overall financial equation. Young people entering the work force need to think about having several careers, caring for themselves in retirement, living longer, and possibly caring for their parents.

In a January 28, 1998, speech at the University of Illinois, President Bill

Clinton said, "There are polls that say young people in their 20s think it's more likely that they will see UFOs than that they will ever collect Social Security."

These young people are probably correct.

The Social Security Administration (www.ssa.gov) claims that for an average retiree in 2010 (these are people getting Social Security now), only 37 percent of his or her income comes from Social Security:

1. 18 percent is from pensions (and those are getting scarcer by the day).

2. 30 percent is from earnings (so some "retirees" are still working).

3. 11 percent is from asset income (investments or real estate).

4. 4 percent is from other public assistance.

Clearly, we cannot rely on Social Security alone to support us in retirement.

Typically, people in their early 20s do not have a plan for their money. They do not save money, and they often do not think of what they will want or need in the future.

The following are popular reasons for ignoring finances:

- Retirement seems like a very long way away.

- They can still call mommy and daddy to bail them out of financial messes.

- They mistakenly believe that they do not earn enough money to be able to save.

- They think, "why bother?"

- There is a mentality that demands "Have fun now!"

- Spending money is enjoyable.

- The future is uncertain.

- They don't know how to save because their parents did not save.

- They don't know how to invest because their parents did not invest.

Ultimately, money is a tool to get what you want and to allow you to do good things for others. But you work all of your life to make an income, and if you don't know what you are doing with your money, you will have nothing to show for your hard work.

Wealth and comfort are attainable goals if you start early. Starting early allows you to make mistakes and recover from those bad decisions.

There are dangers in not planning for the future, such as being impoverished at age 75 and not being able to work.

I know a man who retired as a day laborer when he was 58 years old. Tragedy struck at 61, when he lost his wife to cancer. The medical bills bankrupted him. Now, at 63 years old, with crippling arthritis, he is trying to find a job. He can no longer perform the physically demanding construction work that he used to do for his livelihood. He is applying for jobs that pay only minimum wage.

It is possible to plan for these kinds of events. The younger you are when you start planning, the easier and less costly it is to implement the plan.

This book is designed to help people in their 20s and early 30s plan and maintain financial independence.

There are 15 main points with several follow-up points in each chapter. There are also weblinks to helpful websites for free budgets, plans, inventories, and other helpful tips. Start planning now!

Chapter 2

How to Pay Yourself First

Start a "see ya" fund. Save 6 months worth of expenses so you are never stuck working for someone unethical or mean. With savings, you can tell anyone, "See ya!"

—Linda Byars Swindling
www.LindaSwindling.com

Pay yourself first. Save 10 percent of your gross income. It is really that simple.

The habit of saving 10 percent of your total pay is critical to wealth-building.

Virtually all financial gurus and their books advise people to save 10 percent of what they make. Everyone agrees that you need to start your spending plan by paying yourself first.

There is a difference between saving and investing. Investing is spending money in order to make money. Saving is not spending. Put another way, saving is conserving capital. Investing is reallocating capital to areas that have the potential to grow. In this chapter we focus on saving. We will talk about investing in Chapter 7.

It is a good idea to save 10 percent of your income for long-term needs such as retirement. Plan on saving an additional 10 percent for short-term needs, such as your trip to Nepal or replacing the washing machine.

By saving 10 percent of your gross income (your income before taxes), you ensure that you will take that 10 percent and not spend it. Ideally, you invest this for your retirement and start the critical step to building wealth.

It is not what you make; it is what you save that makes the biggest difference in building wealth.

Setting aside money before you start to spend money on new bills and other expenses ensures that you will not miss the saved money. Some have made the decision to save their pay increases when they receive promotions or pay raises and live on their previous pay until they have built up a comfortable short-term and long-term savings account. Having a robust savings plan solidifies your financial goals and ensures options later.

I am adamant that people take responsibility for their retirement savings. No one wants to be impoverished when they are older.

I recommend saving 10 percent for retirement. This includes money that goes into a 401(k), a 403(B) (if you work for a non-profit organization), an SEP plan, or other types of corporate defined-contribution or defined-benefit plans. It also includes individual retirement plans such as a Roth IRA, a traditional IRA, or military TSP (Thrift Savings Plan).

I also recommend saving another 10 percent so you will have funds available for emergencies, vacations, the down payment on a home, and other unexpected expenses. Interestingly, few people plan for the money they spend on vacations, and then they are surprised when they get home and find they now have vacation credit card debt. Other people are surprised by the Christmas season every year, and then they complain about the bills in January.

Saving that extra 10 percent means you can pay bills when there are surprise expenditures, such as needing to get your car fixed, replacing the refrigerator, or traveling across the country to participate in your best friend's wedding. Recently, a friend told me how she had to replace all four tires on her car after a tire blowout showed that they were all bald. She didn't have the money, so she had to borrow a car until the next payday when she could afford to ransom her car from the tire company. This is a very stressful way to live.

One of the biggest mistakes people make when they first start out is the accumulation of debt for emergencies or even necessities. Having an account designated for large, unexpected items prevents you from getting into this financial sinkhole. This is typically referred to as an "Emergency Fund," and most financial planners recommend having three to six months of your income in this fund.

Some readers, by this point, are already calculating what is left of their salary. Remember that in your beginning earning years, your federal and state taxes are probably going to be less than 15 percent of your income.

Other income taxes to consider are levied by your state. Seven U.S. states—Alaska, Florida, Nevada, South Dakota, Texas, Washington, and Wyoming—have no state income tax. Depending upon where you live, property taxes can be very expensive (such as in New York) or very inexpensive (as in Oklahoma).

Chapter 3

Developing Your Spending and Saving Plan

Want to see into your future?
Look at your budget!

—Cass Mullane
www.prospercreatively.com

Make a spending and saving plan. Many people call this a budget, but budgets tend to have a bad reputation. I encourage people to view this as a monthly spending and saving plan.

Think about it. When do you ever embark on a serious journey (or spring break) without a plan? Successful businesses do not start and stay successful without a business plan, and neither do personal finances.

You spend all of your life preparing to get a job, then working at that job to make money, so why wouldn't you spend a little time getting smarter about managing the money you make?

For some, the idea of setting up a budget sounds as though someone is telling them what *not* to do with their money. That is not true. In fact, by taking control now you are ensuring that you are spending money on things that you really need and not wasting money on things that you don't.

If you have ever worked at a job where you make an hourly wage, you know the value of money. You probably do not waste money foolishly.

Fewer than 10 percent of people claim to use a budget (and those 10 percent are probably just trying to impress the pollsters). In truth, most people spend money throughout the month until it runs out, and then they wait for the next paycheck. This is not good planning.

Some people think that as soon as they get the next promotion, they will be able to save money. Then the pay raise happens. There always seem to be more bills, more commitments, and somehow, despite the pay raise, the financial situation doesn't get better.

According to CreditCards.com, the average annual credit card balance in March 2013 for households with credit card debt is $15,799. The average Annual Percentage Rate (APR) on cards with a balance is 13.1 percent . Even worse, only 40 percent of credit cards are paid off each month.

With 54.8 percent of American households making less than $50,000 per year, it is important to be smart about where one's hard-earned money goes. Paying credit card fees for fleeting purchases is not smart.

Have you ever heard, "I just don't know where the money goes"? Not understanding where we spend is a common problem. Budgets are largely ineffective because people don't know how much they are spending now. So how do you start?

The first step is to figure out what your spending priorities are. How? Try this for one month to determine where your money goes. Every evening, everyone in the house records what they spent money on that day, down to the penny, by category. If you are single, this is easy because you have no one to worry about but yourself. If you're in a relationship or you have a family, you must incorporate the family. Every member of the family participates fully and honestly. Here are some suggested categories:

- Groceries

- Clothing/laundry
- Rent/mortgage
- Electricity
- Telephone
- Cellular phone
- Home maintenance
- Household expenses
- Vehicle expenses
- Gas
- Car insurance
- Home insurance
- Loans
- Education
- Entertainment
- Dining out/lunches/personal care

- Gifts
- Pets
- Savings/investments
- Childcare
- Donations
- Taxes
- Medical expenses
- Dental care
- Miscellaneous

After one month, you will have a good idea of where your money goes. (For a free, downloadable interactive budget sheet, go to http://www.productiveleaders.com/free-stuff.)

Many people protest that during this month there were *special items*. "But this month wasn't normal." "There were birthdays, a work trip; the car needed fixing," and all kinds of other excuses. None of that matters.

There is no such thing as a normal month. There will always be holidays, birthdays, accidents, and "special" situations every month. Just keep track of all of the expenditures for a month and you'll be able

to see where the money is going.

Wealth-building tip: For three months, track every penny your entire household spends. Every cent. You'll be amazed at how quickly savings add up when you are paying attention and are accountable to someone else.

The other big advantage to tracking all of your expenditures in the "one month only" program is that people tend to be far more judicious if they know they have to confess their spending each evening. Do you really want your partner to know you bought that candy bar, or yet another pair of shoes?

CASH OR CREDIT?: Another good way to continue to track expenditures is to use the "all cash or all credit method."

The credit method is to charge every expense on one single credit card. When the statement arrives, you can see where the money went. This works if you pay off that card *in full* every month; otherwise, you are just creating more debt.

The cash method is to pay cash for everything. Put your monthly cash in an envelope, and religiously record every single penny spent on the envelope. Spend $1 on a soda? Write it on the envelope.

For some, carrying limited amounts of cash while keeping their credit cards in a plastic glass filled with water in their freezer is enough to curb credit card spending impulses. For others, cash in the wallet magically disappears. For them, the credit card method is advisable. The caveat here is that when you utilize a credit card, studies show you spend more because you don't "feel" the money leaving you. Flipping a credit card onto a counter registers nothing emotionally.

A study of credit card use at McDonald's found that **people spent 47 percent more** when using credit instead of cash. This is money you could have saved. (See http://www.daveramsey.com/article/the-truth-about-credit-card-debt.)

Mary's Note: Not sure about how you spend? Put a $100 bill in your wallet. Do you rush to break that $100? If so, carrying cash is dangerous for you.

When we first got Rudder, our dog, we got a dog bed, crate, brushes, shampoo, toys, collars, and leashes, and of course we had to take her to the vet to get shots and checkups. The first month (not including the price of the actual dog), we spent over $500 on the dog. (Yes, I know that sounds a little crazy to some people, but I'm fine with that.) But yes, even we were surprised at how much that puppy cost. I understand that people with babies have similar experiences. (More on family budgets in Chapter 15.)

GET AN ALLOWANCE: In any beginning budget, the "miscellaneous" category winds up being larger than most people realize. Events without categories pop up, and they cost money. So assign a category named "miscellaneous" and designate a dollar amount for it. This works especially well if you have older children.

If every member of the family agrees to adhere to his or her particular allowance, then parents are not bombarded by repeated requests. Additionally, children get an early chance to be smart about money. Children learn early that something they want must come out of the allowance or it doesn't happen.

Allowances work for adults too, since it requires them to pay attention to those miscellaneous $10 here and there, which add up to hundreds or thousands of dollars every year.

Being smart about money doesn't mean depriving yourself or your family of what you really want. It's about knowing where the money goes and making the most of what you have.

Part of developing a spending and saving plan is making sure you have the resources to get what you want. As the author of *Do It*, Peter McWilliams writes, "You can have anything you want; you just can't have everything you want." The purpose behind developing a spending and saving plan is to make sure that you get the things you want, and not accumulate a bunch of junk you don't need.

Money is just a tool to get what you want. Managing that money means managing your wants and needs.

I am not going to advise people to give up lattes or stop buying gas or cut back on going out with your friends. But I am going to tell you that without a plan, money falls through your hands like water.

Budgeting Idea: One way to save money and live on a budget without having to keep a meticulous account every month is to first determine what your monthly budget need is. Yes, you have to keep a careful budget for at least one month.

1. Deposit all of your income into a savings account.

2. Have the savings account automatically transfer your monthly budgeted amount into your checking account for the month. For example, let's say you have $4,000 of income. That goes into your savings account. If you are trying to live on $3,500, then that

amount gets transferred to your checking account for the month.

3. Take all expenses out of that checking account.

4. Fine-tune until you are balanced. If you continue to spend down your checking account to the point you need to make additional transfers from savings, then you know your budget isn't right and you need to adjust it.

Once you have it balanced, you see your savings account grow, and those funds can then be used for emergencies

or to make transfers into your
investment accounts.

Money $mart

Chapter 4

Taxes

It isn't what you make,
it is what you keep.

—Rich Tilghman

You need to know what you make *after* taxes so you can effectively make a spending plan.

A very successful lawyer told me that he never understood why he and his family always seemed short of money. "I make $200,000 per year," he confided. "I think that is a really good income. But we never seem to have any money, and we have $100,000 in debt."

He was generating $200,000 per year, but between federal and state taxes, he is paying 30 percent, or $60,000 per year, in income taxes. His property taxes were another $5,000, so right off the top, before he and his family can start budgeting for their expenses, they have to take into account that they only have $135,000 to spend.

This is good money, but his family was budgeting for $200,000 of disposable income (the income you get to keep after taxes), which they did not have.

Every year they were overspending by $65,000 and not understanding why. Their yearly budget had a deficit of $65,000, so in three years they accumulated $195,000 in debt. Yikes!

This is the difference between deficit and debt. Deficit spending is over-spending, and debt is the end result of adding up the deficits plus interest.

Let's start by figuring out how much you make. Pull out your income statements for the last year and determine what you make before taxes (your gross income) and what you make after taxes are subtracted (your disposable income). This sounds basic, but many people truly don't know how to do it.

Disposable income is the money you make and get to keep after you pay taxes. If you're working for someone else, this is fairly easy because they automatically withhold your federal and state taxes, Medicare, and Social Security.

There are many other taxes that we pay in the United States. While they vary by location, they may include sales tax, capital gains tax, inheritance tax, tolls, cigarette and tobacco tax, gasoline tax, alcoholic beverage tax, real property transfer tax, car registration tax, hotel room occupancy tax, gambling tax, air transportation tax, and gift tax, among others.

When you create a spending and saving plan, you have to consider these taxes, too, and budget for them.

When you are in your first jobs, you will probably be in a fairly low tax bracket. Your tax bracket will increase as you gain more experience and more income. In the United States, federal income taxes are considered progressive. This means that as your income goes up, you are taxed at a gradually increasing percentage rate of your income. About half of all Americans pay no federal income tax at all, due to the marginal tax structure.

Mary's Note: The top 5 percent of income-generating people pay 58 percent of all federal taxes collected in the US as of 2012.

In order to build wealth, it is important to understand the difference between pre-tax investments, such as a 401(k) or a traditional IRA (Individual Retirement Account), and investments that are made after you have already paid tax on your income, such as a Roth Individual Retirement Account. There is more on this in the chapter on retirement.

Chapter 5

Why You Must Start Now:
The Magic of Compound Interest

Compound interest is where math suddenly becomes interesting. Many people have a list of reasons why they do not save money. Excuses range from a feeling of entitlement and a desire to have fun now to not knowing where to start. Some claim that they don't make enough money to save. The list goes on and on, but considering the off-chance that you won't die early, you need to make sure that you will be comfortable in your later earning years.

You need to start now. Why? It's simple: The magic of compound interest. Albert Einstein is credited with saying, "Compound interest is the most powerful force in the world."

Here's why. Let's say you're 20 years old and you are going to start saving $50 per month. You put this money in a mutual fund generating eight percent per year. The mutual fund is in your Roth Individual Retirement Account (Roth IRA). A Roth IRA lets you make withdrawals from your IRA tax-free. That means you do not have to pay taxes on this money when you begin withdrawals.

If you continue to add $50 a month, by the time you're 50 you will have $75,561. If you continue this practice for just another 10 years, by the time you're 60, this nest egg has more than doubled to $176,922.

Let's pretend that throughout your earning years you never change the $50 that you continue to add to this account. (I am confident that you will able to afford much more as you get older, but for the sake of this illustration let's just stick with $50 per month.) By the time you are 70, after contributing just $50 per month at an eight-percent rate of return per year for 50 years, you will have $401,924.

If you can find a way to get a 12-percent rate of return over time with just $50 invested each month for 50 years, you are looking at $1,992,025. However, if you wait 10 years before you started investing, you only have $600,053. If you think you're going to live past 100, and you invested for 60 years, on your 88th birthday you might be able to look forward to $6,586,071.

These 10 years make a huge difference in the world of compound interest. Still not convinced? If you had started investing $50 per month when you were 20 years old with an 8-percent rate of return until you were 70, you would have $901,335.

If you found a 20-percent rate of return, that same $50 per month invested for 50 years is now $62.8 million.

Caution: Is it reasonable to expect 20 percent? No. Can you get it occasionally? Yes. We can get lucky sometimes. But don't get discouraged

if your returns are not spectacular.
Spectacular results are hard to get.

Find that extra money every month to
invest.

Chapter 6

How to Find Extra Cash When the Couch Cushions Come Up Empty

Most of these strategies involve ways to find money on a tight budget, so if you already have plenty of money, feel free to skip this chapter. For many people, finding that extra $50 per month is hard. It is really hard if you have never had to limit your spending before now. (Goodbye, Bank of Mommy and Daddy. Hello, reality.)

Saving money is good for you.

1. **Keep us from temptation.** Stay away from shopping malls, garage sales, and swap meets. Keep driving past the strip malls and stores instead of stopping. Turn off the computer and late-night advertising shows. Especially shy away from those home parties thrown with the intent of selling you products. If you don't put yourself in the situation where you are able to spend money, you won't.

2. **Just say no to solicitations.** We all love to support the soccer team,

the band, and the school field trip, but if you don't really need the cookies or the chili, be strong. Think of your own welfare. Smile nicely and say, "Thanks, but no thanks."

3. **Mary's Note:** I do buy Girl Scout cookies, but when I feel I have already purchased my fair share (and already bought cookies for all of my students), I smile knowingly and tell the cookie-wielding table

attendants I have my own Girl Scout. (I do make it a rule not to lie deliberately to children, so I mumble the word "uniform." In my defense, I was a Brownie once— does that count?).

4. **Avoid making any purchases from a television advertisement or shopping channel or through the Internet.** It is easy to spend money carelessly. Infomercials and television salespeople are good at their jobs, which is to create a desire for their product. You don't really need whatever it is. Very

few absolute necessities are sold
for $19.95 plus shipping and
handling.

5. **Recognize your buying behavior.**
Many people shop when they are
bored, hungry, tired, or upset. This
makes them susceptible to
unnecessary impulse buys. Don't
do it!

6. **Differentiate between just-wants
and true needs.** If you really want
something and you can afford it,
wait 24 hours and then go back to
get it. You may find that with time
to think, you may not really want

it enough to make a trip back to make the purchase. You'll be amazed at what you forget to buy because it isn't that important. Yes, new lawn chairs would be nice, but they can wait until next year.

7. **If you can't afford it, don't buy it.** Don't buy something you don't truly need to live when you're living on a tight budget.

8. **Picture the garage sale.** Think about what that item would sell for at a garage sale. Do you really want it for its current price?

9. **Buy a shirt, toss a shirt.** For a short time, I lived on a sailboat. There is very limited storage on a boat. The rule was that if you bought something, then something else had to go because there simply was no space. So if you bought a shirt, you had to think about what shirt you were going to toss.

10. **Mary's hanger technique.** Another trick is to buy a certain number of plastic hangers. Hang up all of your clothes. If you run out

of hangers, you know something has to go.

11. **Make it a team effort.** Even small children need to understand they do not get everything they want. Many parents would rather give in than say no to their children in public. If children are part of the budget decisions, they understand why they don't get every new toy or gadget they see. This is good life training.

Mary's Note: Many young people are over-indulged by well-meaning parents. This creates two problems:

- The child, even at 27, believes he or she is entitled to anything and everything he or she wants.

- The parents, as a result of indulging their children, have not adequately saved for their own retirement.

Dear Young People,

You can have stuff now, but you need to know your parents will be moving in with you when they run out of money. Just saying...

Love,
Your Parents

Money $mart

Chapter 7

Investing for the Future:
Avoid Buying Cat Food
When You Don't Have a Cat

One of my friends once shared that she was afraid of the risks associated with the stock market, stocks, bonds, and mutual funds. "I don't understand the stock market," she confided, "and I am afraid of losing everything I've worked for."

I said, "I am afraid of being old and buying cat food when I don't own a cat."

Human beings can live on cat food for long periods of time. It has a very high protein content, and it is digestible, so I've heard. I'm not advocating that you try to survive on cat food. This whole book is dedicated to you *not* living on cat food.

The point is, don't resort to con-suming cat food or other inexpensive sources of food to stay alive because you are broke.

If you are saving 10 percent of your income you need to know what to do with it. Your next step is determining where you will invest it. Investing is spending money in order to make more money.

I firmly believe that most people should be safely tucked into several mutual funds before they venture into individual stocks.

Mutual funds are a pool of funds collected from many investors and invested in stocks, bonds, money markets, and securities. Many have a theme, such as science and technology, precious metals, or healthcare, or they focus on an investing goal, such as generating income or growth. Mutual funds have fund managers who decide what to add to the mutual fund portfolio. Mutual funds give investors a wide variety of options for a diversified portfolio that ideally carries a lower risk than individual stocks or bonds.

A stock is also known as an equity or a share. It is a portion of the ownership of a corporation, which gives the stock's owner a stake in the company and its profits. For example, if a corporation issues 100 stocks, then each stock represents a one-percent ownership in the company. Stocks are issued when a company goes "public" at an initial public offering. Some stocks pay dividends every quarter or year, based on the profits made for that period of time.

Bonds are IOUs. You buy a bond at a fixed price, and they pay you a specific amount later. A bond is a fixed-interest asset issued by governments, companies, banks, public utilities, and other large entities. There are many different kinds of bonds. For example, a discount bond pays the bond owner, or bearer, only at the ending date, while a coupon bond pays the bearer a fixed amount over a specified interval (every month, year, etc.) as well as paying a fixed amount at the end date.

Know what you are investing in before you buy into something. If you understand the food industry and you believe the people will always purchase certain types of foods, then maybe think about investing money in a certain food provider.

It helps to understand the companies you are investing in. If it is a company that you don't understand making a product that you would never use or don't understand, don't buy it.

Mary's Quick Note: If you can't explain it, don't buy it.

How do we invest in the market? Answer: Buy low and sell high.

This sounds very basic, and it is. However, most people don't do it. They follow other people in the market. People are sheep, and when one gets scared, the others panic.

As a result, when the market drops, many investors tend to sell. When the market is high, their confidence resumes and they tend to buy. It is mathematically foolish to buy at a premium and sell at a loss. This is like waiting until you get on cruise ship to buy a bathing suit when you can see what everyone else is wearing. You are paying a high price to look like everyone else on the cruise.

If a company has good fundamentals, then when the market goes down, you buy more because those stocks are on sale. However, I do not advise you to try to "time" the market. Most people lose when they try to do this. While it is preferable to always buy low and sell high, reality proves that "market-timing" is difficult. Even the professional money managers don't time the market.

So how *do* we take advantage of the highs and lows of the market?

Dollar cost averaging is sustained, regular investments over the long term.

Dollar cost averaging is allocating a specific amount of money to your investment portfolio at regular intervals instead of making one purchase of stocks or funds all at once and hoping you didn't buy at a high.

Dollar cost averaging ensures that investment dollars are spread across periods of both low and high stock or mutual-fund prices. Dollar cost averaging means that when a stock or mutual-fund price is high, you automatically buy fewer shares at that time. If the stock or mutual-fund price is low, you wind up buying more shares at that time.

Example: If you have $100 a month to buy a mutual fund, and one month the mutual fund costs $10, then you buy 10 shares. If the mutual fund is $25, then (because the price is higher) you only buy four shares. If the price drops to $10 per share that means you bought 10 shares, so you get more shares at a lower price.

Watch out for commissions. Commissions are not necessarily evil; however, if you are making an investment you should know if someone else is profiting from your transaction. If someone is getting paid a percentage when you buy or sell, that is a commission.

There are frontloaded, back-loaded, and level-loaded funds. Frontloaded funds mean that you pay a commission when you first get into the fund. Back-loaded funds mean you pay a commission when you withdraw money from the fund. Level-loaded funds mean you don't pay a commission to buy or a commission to sell (as long as you hold the fund for at least one year), but your operating expenses are higher for as long as you own the fund.

Both front- and back-loaded funds are designed to keep you in the fund. Why? Sheep-like behavior is bad for investing. When the market goes down and stocks are cheaper, that is exactly when mutual-fund managers want to scoop up

Money $mart

more shares of companies that are "on sale." But they can't, because when the market drops, people panic, and they sell their mutual fund shares (even if it is at a loss). So to pay off those people who are scared, at the exact time when the fund managers want to be buying more shares, instead they have to sell (at the low price), which reduces overall profit.

Be smart about your investments. You do not have to become the world's greatest financial analyst; however, you should take an active interest in managing your portfolio. Do not blindly turn your investments over to anyone else. At the very least, review your portfolio once a year and make sure that you understand the investments you are in. If you don't understand, ask questions until you do.

If an investment makes you queasy, you should not be in that investment.

Find a financial advisor you can trust, if you are going to use one, and get rid of the companies that you don't understand. The key to wise investing is to know why you own what you own. If you don't know why you own it, you should not have it in your portfolio.

Chapter 8

Know Your Debt, and Work to Eliminate Bad Debt Forever

Pay a little extra principle each month on a loan and you are buying freedom from that loan sooner. I paid off my school loan ten years early!

—Robin Neal
www.Nealresources.com

Get rid of debt. Work harder to stop spending on stupid stuff. Seriously. Debt due to frivolous purchases is the number-one reason young adults get into money trouble.

Some advisors and entrepreneurs classify debt as either "good debt" or "bad debt." House debt is called a mortgage. This debt, if you purchase wisely, is "good debt" because it is building equity, as long as you are in a given location for three to five years. There is nothing wrong with renting longer before making this very important decision.

Bad debt is debt that you carry on your credit card for more than a month for anything that is not an absolute necessity. For example, if the washing machine breaks, the new washing

machine on a credit card is acceptable. But if it takes more than three
months to pay it off, you probably
have bad debt.

If you're going out to eat and you need
to put that meal on a credit card that
you will not be able to pay off in full at
the end of the month, that is bad debt.

Good Versus Bad Debt

A house that you live in with a
mortgage is probably good debt.

A car that you can afford is acceptable
debt. A car that costs more than four
to five times your monthly salary is
probably not good debt. That is a more

expensive car than you really need. What you need in a car is reliable transportation. Everything after that is just a want.

One technique commonly used by car salesmen is to ask, "How much do you want to pay per month?" Then they decide the kind of car to show you.

Commercials tout the monthly cost to buy (the initial cost over 60-72 monthly payments) or lease a car. The question you should ask yourself is, "Can I afford the cost of the entire car?" It is best to buy a used car you can afford and then save for a better car until you get the car you want *and* can afford.

Tracking Your Debt

Get all of your bills together for the month. As you make a payment, make a list:

Credit Card	Amount Paid	Balance Remaining	APR
Visa	$100	$2,190	7.9%
MasterCard	$75	$1,100	13.9%
Specialty card	$25	$125	18.1%
Total:		*$3,415*	

If you make a quick list, you find that you need to pay the specialty card off as soon as possible because it has the highest APR (annual percentage rate). The annual percentage rate is the interest you pay.

Every month take the total amount of debt, in this case $3,415, and write it on a Post-It note on the refrigerator. Also, write it down on your calendar. I suggest writing it down on the last day of the month.

Every month, track that debt number to see how well you are working to eliminate debt. It is motivating to see your debt go down!

Chapter 9

The American Dream:
Your House—Owning or Renting?

You are on your own, so where should you live? Many American people view buying a home as a terrific investment.

Mary's Note: I like real estate. I like owning homes as a source of income, but I have also seen sad cases where people lose their savings and investments because of poor real-estate decisions.

Yes, I know the market fluctuates up and down, which means a lot of real estate is on sale. Many homes are deeply discounted right now as well. For most Americans, owning their own home is their largest source of wealth accumulation, so buy wisely.

Mary's Rule: Don't buy unless you are going to be in a given location for three to five years.

If you are not going to live in a location for more than three years, do a *very* careful cost-benefit analysis of the commissions, homeowners association fees, sales taxes, property maintenance, escrow fees, etc., before taking the leap into home ownership. As many people have discovered over the past decade, real-estate valuations do not always go up.

Owning your own home can also have great tax benefits for both your own home and, possibly, rental property.

The concept of home ownership is easy. Choose a home, write a contract, put some money down, and borrow the rest of the money you need as a home loan or mortgage. Pay off the mortgage in 30 years, and live in the home another 30 or 40 years. Then sell the home to pay for retirement living.

For years, Americans mistakenly believed that home prices constantly increased. The subprime mortgage crisis caused housing prices to fall in many areas and destabilized the housing market. Many people lost wealth. (For more information on how the subprime lending issues caused the mortgage meltdown, visit www.crisisofcredit.com. It's a cartoon. You'll like it.)

Real estate can be a great wealth-building tool. For most people, buying and living in their own homes is a sound financial decision, but there are some points to consider.

The short course in being smart about real estate has the following rules:

1. Buy a house you are comfortable living in for a long time.

2. Buy a house in a location where you want to live for a long time.

3. Be able to afford the payments and the maintenance on the home you buy.

4. Remember that you will always be able to rent more "house" (more space, amenities, etc.) for the same money than what you can buy in terms of monthly payments.

Here is the longer course in being smart in real estate.

Do not buy a home unless you're going to be in that area for three to five years. You can press the "I believe" button now, and skip to the next section, but if you want more of an explanation, continue reading.

When you buy a house, you might be delighted to learn that generally the seller pays the commission—the cost of both their real estate agent and yours. In most states, this translates to about six to seven percent of the selling price of the house. So at six percent for a $200,000 house, the sellers are going to have to pay $12,000 to real estate agents. (This seems like a lot of money, and it is, but I think great real estate agents are well worth the cost. Mary's disclaimer: Yes, I have an inactive real-estate license.)

You, as the buyer, have to come up with (usually) a 20-percent down payment—in this case, $40,000—to secure your home loan or mortgage. You'll probably also need to pay another one percent in escrow fees, so add in another $2,000 on that $200,000 home. Then you have to consider taxes. Escrow, the people who do all of the accounting when a home is transferred, will prorate your property taxes for the rest of that calendar year. But in many states, you also have to pay a tax so that the state will record the sale and transfer the title to you. (You don't have a choice. Otherwise you don't get "recorded," and you don't legally own the house.)

Here is an example of how taxes affect your buying decision:

Let's say you buy a house in Baltimore, Maryland. The state of Maryland assesses 0.5 percent in transfer tax, and Baltimore County assesses a 1.5-percent tax. (If you're going to live in the home, in Baltimore County the first $22,000 of the home is exempt from county tax.) A two-percent tax on

$200,000 is another $4,000 that you have to bring to escrow. The recordation tax is $10 per $1,000, so that adds another $2,000 to what you need to bring to escrow. And the property tax is $1.247 per hundred of the assessed value of the house, so if you had to pay for the whole year, that would be another $2,494. So you as a buyer, on a $200,000 house, need to show up with $50,494. You also need to be able to make the monthly payments of principle, interest, taxes, and mortgage insurance (if required).

When you sell the house you have to remember that homes do not sell instantly. If you need to move in June, you should start selling your house in January of that year. If it sells quickly, then you have to live in a temporary place for a few months. This costs both time and money. If the house does not sell, you are stuck with paying for a house that you do not live in.

Most people who buy homes take a few months to find the right house, and if you need to start selling your house six months before you intend to move, you may only be really living in the house for two years.

When you sell the house, you are responsible for paying the 6 percent commission rate to the real estate agents, plus another 1 percent to escrow. So even if the home price goes up by 5 percent by the time you sell the house, making your selling price $210,000, just the logistics of selling the house is still going to cost you $14,700. You'll probably also have to repaint, re-carpet, and perform a variety of other things tasks to make your home attractive to buyers. This, again, takes both time and money.

So unless the house is in a location where you will be returning to and you want to live there at a later time, to make buying a house worthwhile, you should plan on being in the house for three to five years.

You need to be able to afford all of the costs of home ownership. The combination of the monthly payments plus utilities, taxes, and other maintenance should not exceed 35 percent of your income. In order to qualify for a home mortgage, one of the standard rules is that the monthly mortgage payment (usually including taxes and insurance, if required) cannot exceed 28 percent of your monthly income.

Scenario: If you know that you want to buy a $200,000 house, and you are prepared to put down 20 percent , then you will have to take out a mortgage on $160,000. A 30-year mortgage, assuming a five-percent interest rate, will put the monthly payment at about $859. Over the 30 years, the life of loan, you will pay about $309,000 for that $160,000 loan. You pay $149,209 in interest.

If you do not qualify for the five-percent interest rate (because you didn't pay attention to your FICO score), and instead you get a six-percent interest rate, your monthly payment is now $960 per month, and you'll wind up paying $345,341 over the life of the loan, which is $185,341 in interest for that $160,000 loan.

Trick to saving for a home: Pretend that you are paying the mortgage now. Rent an apartment for $700, and diligently save the extra $149 or $260 per month, or whatever the amount you would be paying if you actually had a mortgage. That gets you used to making those payments and saves for your down payment.

Warning on rental property: Be careful about buying property solely as a rental. Do not buy a house as a co-op rental with friends unless you really know what you are doing. This is a common idea with some young people. They think real estate is an easy and profitable investment because they often don't understand all of the costs. Buying property and renting it is a business endeavor and should be treated as such.

According to government statistics, most rental property is rented out only about five months of every year, and most rental property only yields about a two- to three-percent rate of return per year, and that's once you start making money. It generally takes several years of property ownership before you start turning a property rental into profit.

Having a rental property means that you are responsible for all mortgage payments, taxes, maintenance, and insurance. Then you have to find someone who wants to rent it or hire a property manager. A property manager generally costs between 10 and 20 percent of the monthly rent, and that does not cover the cost of repairs.

Should you rent? At times, yes. You are almost always going to be able to rent more house for the money than what you can afford to buy. Renting has several significant benefits. You do not have to pay taxes or maintenance fees or perform maintenance work, and you can probably afford to live in a housing area with a good school district that you might not be able to afford if you were buying a house. If you are in a job that requires you to move, such as the military, renting is frequently the best option, considering deployments, early permanent change of station, and other uncertainties.

A note on mortgages: You should get a fixed-rate mortgage 99 percent of the time. If you can manage the payments, get a 15-year mortgage as opposed to a 30-year mortgage. Trust me. (But do the math anyway.)

One of my favorite books on buying and selling homes is *The Idiot's Guide to Buying and Selling a House* by Peter

Richmond, published by the Penguin Group. Another great book is *Not One Dollar More*, by Joseph Eamon Cummins.

Home ownership can be a good investment and has many benefits. Being smart when buying your house makes your home a great investment.

Chapter 10

Cars: Buying Versus Leasing

My car has a high PF factor. Paid for.

—Terry Brock

www.TerryBrock.com

Buying a car is both exciting and scary. Most working adults in America will need a car. If you need a car, you should generally buy rather than lease a car.

Mary's Caveat: One of the few times you might need to lease a car is if you are using the car strictly for business and your accountant tells you to for ease of tax accountability. For the rest of us, buying is the better of the two options.

Buy used: I'm opposed to buying new cars unless you can basically pay cash for them. That means you can afford the car.

New cars depreciate as soon as you drive them off the lot. Generally speaking, buying a car that is at least a year or two old is a better value. During our latest recession, so many people were flocking to buy used cars that new cars were actually a better deal, so consider the economy when you consider the car market.

What You Need Versus What You Want

Quality in a car is a completely subjective issue. Do you care about acceleration or safety? Gas mileage or storage space? A sunroof or a ski rack? A truck bed or an SUV? Built-in child seats or built-in surround sound?

Before you even think about going shopping for a car, consider what you actually *need* in a vehicle. If you are starting a family, you may not want to admit it, but doors that slide open on both sides are exceedingly handy.

When I shop for a car I look for a few basic things: four-wheel drive, plenty of space in the back for all of my business materials, a front seat with handy cup holders, and convenient storage space. Your criteria will probably be different. Know what you absolutely need to have in a vehicle, and shop for the best value. Look at consumer reports for reliability, safety, gas mileage, and resale value.

If there are informal car lots where you live (they are often called lemon lots, but I have found great cars there), check them out. People park their cars and post signs to sell them. These cars can be very good deals as people have to sell their cars for, for example, a move, a change in a family situation, or a military transfer.

When you start shopping for a car, walk around several car lots, both new and used, to see what appeals to you. Drive your friends' cars. If you think you're going to be doing a lot of driving, make sure you know what vehicles are comfortable.

Never let someone talk you into a car that is too expensive for you by quoting low monthly payment options. That is ridiculous. Look at the total purchase price of the car, including taxes and maintenance.

Mary's Car Budget: My general rule of thumb for buying a car is that you should never buy a vehicle that costs more than four to six months of your take-home pay. I tend to be on the conservative side when it comes time to spending money on a car. So if you make $40,000 a year, then you might be looking at a car that costs around $16,000.

When you shop for a car, consider:

1. How much is the insurance going to be? The nicer the car, the more you pay for insurance. If you are a young man, insurance statistics are against you, and you're going to pay a higher price than the rest of us.

2. How much is maintenance going to cost? The fancier the car, the higher the maintenance costs. Certain car companies make it very difficult for you to take your car

anywhere other than their service departments, and they often have a very high hourly rate to fix your car. It is imperative to know what this cost is before you buy the car.

3. Is the car going to be sitting unused for long periods of time? If you are military and you're going to deploy for several months or a year at a time, buying an expensive car does not make sense, especially if it is getting destroyed by sea salt, snow, or high temperatures.

4. Are you going to be moving around a lot and using your car to haul your belongings?

Mary's Note: How to waste money when buying a car:

1. Just go out one weekend and buy a car without doing research.

2. Buy a car spontaneously or because yours just died and you need one right away. (I suggest that you borrow or rent a car for a few days

or weeks so that you get the right car for you and your budget.)

3. Buy a car you cannot afford.

4. Buy a car as a status symbol to impress your friends.

Ultimately, know what you want to spend, and stick to your budget. If you don't know where to start, try one of the national chains such as CarMax so that you do not have to negotiate. You can also use a car-buying service (offered through many banks), or you can do your own research and negotiate directly with car dealers. The Edmunds (http://www.edmunds.com)

is great for getting the TMV (true market value) for new and used cars in your area, as is Kelley Blue Book (http://www.kbb.com).

Chapter 11

Credit Cards

Credit-card companies make money in essentially three ways.

The first is when they charge an interest rate, called an APR (annual percentage rate), which is the interest we pay when we make a purchase and do not pay off our balance in full. The APR is the interest they charge on that borrowed money. Your APR is shown on your credit card statement.

If your annual percentage rate is high (over nine percent) and you have good credit (more on credit/FICO scores in the next chapter), you can call the company that issued your credit card and ask them nicely to lower your Annual Percentage Rate.

Mary's Note: People who answer phones at credit card companies like to be treated nicely. We all do. So be polite to them. Front-line customer service is hard work. They have a tough job, and they have to tell people "no" many times a day. So be nice.

If the person on the other end of the phone cannot help you, remain very polite and kindly ask for someone else. "Is there someone else there who may be able to help me lower my APR?" Sometimes, if your credit scores are borderline, the front-line person or even his or her supervisor cannot say "yes." You can also ask if there is a better time for you to call back, perhaps during regular working hours. "I really appreciate your help. Is there someone else who might be able to help me another time?"

The second way credit card companies make money is from the fees. These include annual fees, late fees, or awards program type fees, and an ever-increasing amount of other fees for various services or payment methods.

The third and most profitable way credit card companies make money is from your purchases. Merchants (sellers) pay credit card issuers a percentage of your purchase for the privilege of allowing you to use a credit card to buy their items. Visa and MasterCard typically charge around three percent. American Express charges merchants six percent. This is why if you use cash you can sometimes ask for a cash discount and get it; however, in some states, such as Colorado, it is illegal to change the price based on the form of payment.

Mary's Advice: Find a card with a terrific rewards program, so you can benefit from some of those charges.

Mary's Cards: I have several credit cards. I use one Visa as a business card; all of my business purchases go on that card. This card offers the benefit of no overseas transaction fees. I have another card just for personal use. I use yet another card as a backup and for my non-profit expenses. This allows me to keep purchases separate, which is very handy at tax time.

The Grace Period

Many people think they have an entire month of a "grace period" for purchases. Most consumers believe that if they buy a washing machine on September 2, they have until the statement arrives at the end of the month to pay that bill without being charged. That is only true if you carry a zero balance on your card from the month before. For example, if you have $120 still left from your August bill, you have *zero* grace period for any purchases made in September until you pay off the balance of that credit card. Many people think that every new purchase brings with it a whole new "grace period." That is not the case. As a result, many people are surprised when a big-ticket item, such as that television they purchased, starts accruing interest right away.

Should you have a credit card? Yes! Credit cards help you build your credit score (more in Chapter 12 on credit scores), and it is almost impossible to buy an airline ticket or rent a car without one. I think you need two: a primary card and a backup. Sometimes cards fail. Be prepared.

For many people who have not yet compiled an emergency fund, a credit card functions as their emergency fund. When you need new tires or you get caught in a snowstorm and need a hotel room or you have to bail your roommate out of jail (yes, I've done all of those), it is handy to have access to a healthy line of credit.

However, this is a dangerous road to go down because then you rely on the credit card for the monthly "emergency" that always comes up.

"Wow, the kids grew and need new clothes...who knew?" Emergency!

"Wow, Christmas is in December again...who knew?" Let's use the credit cards!

Better to put $1,000 in an emergency fund before any sort of investing or retirement contributions and have that be the emergency fund.

Credit cards are a valuable and necessary tool in today's world. Being smart about how you use credit cards is an important wealth-management tool. If you have a credit card with a low APR, that is the card you should use if you do happen to have unexpected expenses and you do not think you'll be able to pay off the balance at the end of that month.

For your day-to-day expenses that you want to put on a credit card to track your spending, you might want to choose a card that has a terrific rewards program, so you get the incentives such as cash, airline miles, and restaurant gift cards. As long as you pay off the card in full every month, you can choose the rewards program over the APR.

Mary's note on credit cards: Call your credit card issuers if you are going to be traveling outside your normal billing area. Otherwise, they may think the card usage is fraudulent and place a hold on the card. This is for your own protection, but it can be embarrassing if you are hosting a client at dinner and you have to call from Paris to unlock your card.

Credit cards are not money. They need to be paid off. Don't charge what you cannot resolve at the end of the month unless it is a real emergency.

Mary's Observation: I've seen young people use their credit card for a terrific night of partying fun. In some instances, not only does Mr. Life of the Party not remember how much fun he had that night, but he is surprised (not in a good way) when the credit card statement arrives. So, if you think this might be a problem, just carry the cash you intend to spend that night and enough extra cash to take a taxi home. (Yes, I do sound like someone's mom here.)

As of 2013, the average credit card debt for people with credit card debt (about 47 percent of Americans) is over $15,000. The average household income is only $46,000.

Don't get into trouble with credit cards!

Money $mart

Chapter 12

The World of Credit:
Your Permanent Record and
FICO Scores

This is where you do care what other people think about you.

Credit scores are important. If you expect to ever get a loan—for example, to buy a house or a car—and you want a low interest rate, you need to understand the difference between your credit score and your credit report, and how to improve them.

Your credit report consists of your credit history. Your credit score is a three-digit number based on information about you compiled by the three companies in the United States that currently issue credit scores.

The purpose of your credit score is for lenders to determine how responsible you have been with your money. This number helps them decide whether or not they should lend you money, and how much they should charge you.

Your credit report includes information on when you opened a bank account, when you applied for a credit card, what the most recent balance is on your credit cards, how often you make payments on time, and whether or not you have defaulted on any loans. The purpose of the system is to figure out whether or not you will default on loans. The higher your credit score, the better.

The FICO score was developed by Fair, Isaac, and Company, and the scores range from a very low of 300 to a high of 850. Most scores fall in the 600s and 700s, and the average is around 720. As of 2013, to obtain really great lending rates, you need to have a FICO score of 760 or higher.

In 2003, Congress mandated that the three credit agencies—Equifax, Experian, and TransUnion—provide a free credit report annually to each U.S. citizen who requests it. The law does not mandate that they provide the actual credit score. Therefore, for you to learn what your actual credit score is, it will probably cost around $20 to Fair, Isaac, and Company. You can request your credit score for free only if you've been turned down for a loan. The 2010 Finance Reform Bill allows you to get a free copy of the credit score that a potential lender used when evaluating your credit history.

Mary's Note: It is a very good idea to get a copy of your credit report annually. You will be able to check that information is accurate and catch mistakes.

Ways to Improve Your Credit Score

Every time you apply for credit or open a new account, you can reduce your credit score. The "people checking on you" factor accounts for about 10 percent of your total score, so be careful about requesting new credit cards, especially if they are gas cards or credit cards for specific stores, unless you really frequent those retailers.

Never, ever be late with bills. If you travel a great deal, make sure there is some mechanism for automatically paying at least the minimum balance for all of your bills. Your record of paying bills determines about 35 percent of your credit score. Every time you have a late payment your score decreases. The 60-day late payment is worse than a 30-day late payment. The 90-day flag is obviously worse than the 30- or 60-day late flag.

How much debt you have accounts for about 30 percent of your FICO score. The more debt you have *as a percentage of your credit limit*, the worse your score. For example, if you have credit limits on three credit cards of $20,000, and you owe $5,000, that is a 1:4 ratio of debt to credit. That is much better than if you had a credit limit of only $10,000 and still owed the same $5,000, since that would be a 1:2 ratio of debt to credit.

The score likes to see that you have held credit with the same companies for long periods of time. If you routinely close older accounts to open up new ones, this will generally lower your credit score.

Your FICO score will be higher if you have a combination of different kinds of credit. For example, a car loan, a mortgage, and credit cards are a combination of credit types, but FICO is fairly ambiguous about what constitutes the right balance of credit.

The more loans you have with higher balances, the lower your credit score, so make sure that you pay down revolving debt, especially on credit cards with high interest rates.

You might be thinking, "But I'm young—why do I care?" Some young people think they are years away from buying a house and therefore do not need to pay attention to their credit score. However, it is common for landlords, insurance companies, and even prospective employers (and security clearances) to check your credit score even if you are not applying for loans with them.

How do they calculate the score? Roughly, your FICO score is determined as follows:

1. 35 percent: Do you pay bills on time? A late payment will reduce your credit score. Several late payments have a very negative impact on your credit score.

2. 15 percent: The longevity of your credit. The longer you have had credit, the better. I advise people not to cut up their oldest credit card, because hanging onto that

oldest card helps their credit rating. You can keep the card. You don't have to use it.

3. 10 percent: Applying for credit. It sounds counterintuitive, but the more you apply for credit, the more people are asking about your credit, which makes the credit bureaus cranky. Multiple inquiries in a short amount of time will reduce your score.

Mary's Note: This is why you should never, ever apply for a home or any other loan using an Internet-based application process that promises to find your best loan rate with multiple lenders. That company then takes that information and blasts it out to literally hundreds of possible lenders. All of them then swamp the credit bureaus with requests about you. This immediately lowers your credit score and ensures that you will pay a higher interest rate on the loan you wind up obtaining, which is exactly what you are trying to avoid.

4. 10 percent: Types of credit. Having a variety of credit, such as a mortgage, a car loan, and credit cards, is a healthy mix of credit and will increase your credit score.

5. 30 percent: Debt-to-credit ratio. If you have a credit limit of $2,000, and you have $1,000 of debt, that is a 50 percent debt-to-credit ratio. That is bad. If you have a

credit limit of $10,000, and you have $1,000 of debt, that is a 10 percent debt-to-credit ratio. That is good. Again, this is why cutting up credit cards that you don't use is not always a good idea. You may need those cards to increase your credit amount so that your debt-to-credit ratio is lower.

So why should you start checking your credit score now? Credit scores are frequently inaccurate, and you will need to fix those inaccuracies in your records.

Obviously your credit score is important if you're going to buy a car or a house and finance either of those purchases. Your credit score is also important because it will be one of the determining factors in your APR, your annual percentage rate that you pay to your credit card company, if you carry a balance.

What most people don't realize is that your credit score is also used by a variety of other people. Most employers will check your credit score for trustworthiness, reliability, and fiscal responsibility. The U.S. government checks your credit score if you are going to be in a job that requires a security clearance. Landlords will check your credit score to determine whether or not you are a good rental candidate. Your insurance company will also check your credit score when you request insurance.

So how do you build/keep a good credit score?

1. Apply for a credit card. Make sure you pay the bill in full every month.

2. Pay all of your bills on time, including your cell phone bill, your

cable bill, any student loan bills, and anything else that has your name on it with a payment due date.

3. Get a checking account and a savings account at a credit union or a bank with zero or no fees.

4. If you need a car, get a small car loan.

5. Be careful about multiple credit applications. Don't apply for credit just because a store is offering you a free T-shirt, or a blender, or any other gimmick.

6. Don't close old credit card accounts. Keep them active by purchasing a tank of gas occasionally or some other small expense, and pay it off immediately.

7. Pay off debt. Show that you can be responsible with credit.

8. Don't use your credit card if you are going to get anywhere close to your limit unless it is an absolute emergency.

If you know you have bad credit, and you cannot get a credit card, what can you do?

1. Apply for a secured credit card. This type of credit card requires that you keep a certain amount of money on deposit with the company that issued the card. For example, they will give you a $500 credit card, but you have to give them $500 to keep on hold to make sure you pay your bills. Once you develop a pattern of paying your bills, they will increase your credit limit with less money required for a deposit.

2. If you cannot get a regular Visa or MasterCard, you may want to

consider a department store or gas station card, just to start. In general, I do not recommend either of those if you are just starting out, because the multiple inquiries on your credit score will lower your credit score.

3. If your parents have good credit, ask them to add you to a credit card account. If your parents have bad credit, or you are not sure, don't risk it.

One of the easiest ways to check your credit reports is at http://www.annualcreditreport.com.

Fill out the forms and ask for all three reports. To actually buy a copy of your credit score, go directly to the three credit bureaus:

Experian: www.experian.com

Equifax: www.equifax.com

TransUnion: www.transunion.com

Occasionally one or all of the credit bureaus will run a special offering to give you your credit score for just a dollar. This is a good idea. You want to get your hands on your credit report, review it for errors, and correct errors immediately. Common errors include incorrect names, Social Security

Numbers, birth dates, and addresses; accounts that don't belong to you; bad information from over seven years ago; or incorrect entries due to identity theft.

Mary's Note: For years my credit reports decided I that I lived with my parents' neighbors next door, instead of with my parents. My parents denied trying to give me away.

Chapter 13

Life, Health, and Disability Insurance

Life insurance is risk management.

When you purchase a life insurance policy, you are hoping nothing happens to you, but just in case something does, your family has some financial security.

How do you know if you need life insurance? If you have family members who would be impoverished if you die, you need life insurance.

"But I don't think I'm going to die!"

Yes, I remember feeling immortal too. So cheer up, because you have about five times the chance of being disabled than actually dying. Feel better?

Disability insurance is often overlooked. Disability insurance pays out in the event you are unable to work. Short-term disability plans are most commonly available through your employer.

Long-term disability often takes effect after 90 days. Again, plans are most common through your workplace.

Military Note: Military people on active duty are paid their full salary when they are injured and cannot work.

Civilian employers generally stop paying employees if they are not on vacation or sick leave. This is a good reason to consider disability insurance.

Review your life and health insurance policies and programs. If you are part of a company life insurance program, check to make sure that the insurance company that you initially signed up with has not changed and that you have updated your own records as well as updated your beneficiaries. If you are part of a shared health plan, review the options, and know what is covered and what is not. You may need additional coverage.

Chapter 14

Retirement

Retirement is about having enough money to have options when you may not want to work anymore. The lifestyle you will have during your retirement years is largely a function of how disciplined you are from now on.

Your retirement is your responsibility. Many people do not think about retirement until it is too late. The good news is that if you are in your 20s, you have several decades before you need to be living off of your retirement accounts.

Due to compounding interest, the more time you have before you are going to retire, the more risk you can take with the money you put into your retirement accounts. If you are not going to retire for another 50 years, then a market drop for a few years here and there is not going to be of huge concern. However, making sure that your retirement accounts grow enough to keep you well ahead of inflation is also important.

Many parents worry about caring for their children and getting their children off to college to the point that they defer contributing to their own retirement fund. This is a mistake. Children can borrow money to go to college, but you cannot borrow money to be retired.

Your wealth for your retirement years should be divided between your home that you own, your assets, and the money that you have put away specifically for retirement purposes.

Saving now for retirement is the responsible thing to do if you do not want to be buying cat food in your senior years.

How Much Should You Save for Retirement?

Ideally, saving 10 percent of your gross income, the income you make before taxes are taken out, is a good idea for your retirement accounts. This money may be divided among your employer-sponsored account, your Individual Retirement Account (IRA), and some other kinds of retirement options, such as a U.S. government TSP (Thrift Savings Plan).

The U.S. government Thrift Savings Plan (www.TSP.gov) is for civilian employees of the federal government as well as for military personnel. The big difference is that civilian personnel have a funds-matching program, while military people do not.

What Are Your Options for Saving Money for Retirement?

If you have an employer with a retirement plan, that is usually a very good option.

If you have an employer-based plan that matches your contributions into your retirement account, make this your first priority. That means that for every dollar you put into your retirement account, your employer will put in a certain percentage of a dollar. So let's say you put in a dollar, and your employer matches you with $.30. You have immediately made a 30-percent rate of return.

Most of these plans will only match up to a certain dollar or percentage limit, but they are a terrific idea, and you should take advantage of them when you can. After you have contributed the maximum amount to any employer-based plan with a matching program, look at your Individual Retirement Accounts.

Individual Retirement Accounts, or IRAs, come in two different forms. The regular, or traditional, IRA gives you a tax break now, but you pay taxes on the money you put in as well as everything it has made over time when you take it out.

The Roth IRA differs from a traditional IRA in that you do not get a tax break now, but when you pull that money out, the money you put in as well as everything it has generated is tax-free.

Because Roth IRAs are such a good deal, the government places a cap, or an uppermost income limit, on who can contribute to Roth IRAs. As of 2013, a single person can contribute the full amount to a Roth IRA if he or she makes $112,000 or less. If his or her income is between $112,000 and $127,000, they can contribute a declining percentage. If his or her income is greater than $127,000, a person cannot contribute to a Roth IRA.

For married couples in 2013 filing jointly, the new range is an income level of $178,000. Between $178,000 and $188,000, a couple can contribute a percentage. Over $188,000, a married couple filing jointly cannot contribute to their Roth IRAs.

If your income puts you over the limit to contribute to a Roth IRA, employer-based plans become more important. You can also still contribute to a traditional IRA.

Important information about IRAs:

1. Individual Retirement Accounts are exactly that—individual. Your IRA belongs to you; after you, it belongs to whomever you leave as your beneficiary. You do not share your IRA with anyone else. Married

couples do not share IRAs; each person has his or her own IRA.

2. The IRS has a limit on what you can contribute per person per year, and as of 2013, that limit is $5,500. You can generate that $5,500 from multiple sources. For example, your mom can give you $500, and your grandma can give you $100. As long as all of that combined does not exceed $5,500, you are okay. If you go over that amount, the IRS gets involved, sends you a notification, and

makes you take the money out. There's also a fine involved.

3. You can start taking money out of your individual retirement account starting at age 59.5. For a traditional IRA, you must start taking money out of your individual retirement account starting at age 70.5 so that you can start paying taxes on that money.

4. Because the government does not get taxes from your Roth IRA, you do not need to start taking money out of your Roth IRA at any specific time. That money can grow tax-

free forever. You can leave that money to your children or your grandchildren.

5. Many young people balk at the idea of putting money away for the next 30 or 40 years. Retirement seems like a long way away. Plus, we want to have fun now! While it is inadvisable to pull money out of your IRA before you are 59.5, there are provisions to do so.

Taking money out of an IRA generally subjects you to a 10-percent penalty from the federal government, plus whatever your state charges. However, you can avoid early withdrawal penalties in the following situations:

a. You can withdraw money up to $10,000 from an IRA for a first-time home purchase.

b. You can make a withdrawal for higher-education expenses for you, your spouse, your children, or your grandchildren.

c. You can make a withdrawal if you have major medical expenses that exceed 7.5 percent of your income or a disability.

Many company retirement plans allow you to borrow money against your own balance. This is like borrowing money from yourself. The interest payments go back into your account. However, if you do not repay your loan to yourself, the government looks at this as a withdrawal, and you are subject to early withdrawal penalties.

Your IRA is just an account that, by adhering to a few rules, tells the government that that money does not get taxed (in the case of a Roth IRA) or that that money does not get taxed until you start taking it out (in the case of a regular IRA).

You can put a variety of different types of investments into your IRAs. These can be stocks, bonds, or mutual funds, and now you can even purchase a house within your IRA.

If something happens and your life expectancy looks to be shorter than that of the average person, the IRS allows you to withdraw the money before age 59.5 as long as you take the money in equal and annual installments. Check with the IRS—yes, they actually have a chart for looking up your life expectancy.

When should you not be contributing to a retirement account? If you need the money to keep your home or purchase a home, you might need to defer contributing to a retirement account for a period of time. If you lose your job or are back in school, it may be very difficult to think about retirement if you are worried about just getting by.

Mary's guide for retirement accounts:

1. Start saving for retirement now.

2. Have a dedicated fund that you simply do not touch because it is for your retirement.

3. Contribute to your employer-based retirement account as much as possible to benefit from their matching program.

4. Fully fund your Roth IRA.

Confused by retirement and investment options? Hire a financial adviser for help. Many are fee-based, meaning they do not get a percentage of your accounts. Others are commission-based, so they do get a percentage. Find out before you work with them.

Financial planners work for years to be able to call themselves Certified Financial Planners, and they study financial data all the time. Their expertise is well worth the investment.

www.irs.gov/publications/p590/ar01.html

Q&A: How Are Traditional IRAs and Roth IRAs Different?

Is there an age limit on when I can open and contribute to my IRA?

Traditional IRA: Yes. You must not have reached age 70.5 by the year's end. See Who Can Open a Traditional IRA? in Chapter 1.

Roth IRA: No. You can be any age. See *Can You Contribute to a Roth IRA?* in Chapter 2.

If I earned more than $5,000 in 2011 ($6,000 if I was 50 or older by the end *of 2011), is there a limit on how much I can contribute to my IRA?*

Traditional IRA: Yes. For 2011, you can contribute to a traditional IRA up to $5,000, or $6,000 if you were 50 or older by the end of 2011. There is no upper limit on how much you can earn and still contribute. See How Much Can Be Contributed? in Chapter 1.

Roth IRA: Yes. For 2011, you may be able to contribute to a Roth IRA up to $5,000, or $6,000 if you were age 50 or older by the end of 2011, but the amount you can contribute may be less depending on your income, filing status, and if you contribute to another IRA. See How Much Can Be Contributed? and Table 2-1 in Chapter 2.

Can I deduct contributions to my IRA?

Traditional IRA: Yes. You may be able to deduct your contributions depending on your income, filing status, whether you are covered by a retirement plan at work, and whether you receive social security benefits. See How Much Can You Deduct? in Chapter 1.

Roth IRA: No. You can never deduct contributions to a Roth IRA. See *What Is a Roth IRA?* in Chapter 2.

Do I have to file a form just because I contribute to my IRA?

Traditional IRA: Not unless you make non-deductible contributions. In that case, you must file Form 8606. See Non-deductible Contributions in Chapter 1.

Roth IRA: No. You do not have to file a form if you contribute to a Roth IRA. See *Contributions Not Reported* in Chapter 2.

Do I have to start taking distributions when I reach a certain age from my IRA?

Traditional IRA: Yes. You must begin receiving required minimum distributions by April 1 of the year following the year you reach age 70.5. See When Must You Withdraw Assets? (Required Minimum Distributions) in Chapter 1.

Roth IRA: No. If you are the original owner of a Roth IRA, you do not have to take distributions regardless of your age. See *Are Distributions Taxable?* in Chapter 2. However, if you are the beneficiary of a Roth IRA, you may have to take distributions. See *Distributions After Owner's Death* in Chapter 2.

How are distributions taxed from my IRA?

Traditional Distributions from a traditional IRA are taxed as ordinary income, but if you made nondeductible contributions,
not all of the distribution is taxable. See Are Distributions Taxable? in Chapter 1.

Roth IRA: Distributions from a Roth IRA are not taxed as long as you meet certain criteria. See *Are Distributions Taxable?* in Chapter 2.

Do I have to file a form just because I receive distributions from my IRA??

Traditional IRA: Not unless you have ever made a nondeductible contribution to a traditional IRA. If you have, file Form 8606.

Roth IRA: Yes. File Form 8606 if you received distributions from a Roth IRA (other than a rollover, qualified charitable distribution, one-time distribution to fund an HSA, recharacterization, certain qualified distributions, or a return of certain contributions).

Mary's Note: Not everyone is eligible for a ROTH IRA. There are income restrictions.

Chapter 15

Getting Involved, For Better or For Worse: Couples and Money

Kicking that "Grande half caff soy toffee nut latte extra hot (no whip)" crack habit every day equated about $1200-1500 a year savings ... enough for an annual trip to Italy to drink REAL espresso!

—Valerie Caruso
www.vinowithval.com

I often tell my personal finance students that there are three very important things many of us do in life for which we are largely unprepared. We get married or engage in long-term relationships, we have children, and we manage our money. This chapter addresses the first and the third of these important facets of our lives.

Couples often have difficulty talking openly with each other about their finances. There are valid reasons why calm, rational, mutually agreeable money discussions are uncommon. Most of us were never taught to sit down with a pile of bills, the checkbook, and the budget and happily discuss our income and spending for the month over an evening cocktail.

Most Americans grow up without any type of money education. It is far more likely that we learn that discussions on money are forbidden or private because 1) there was never enough of it; 2) children were sheltered from such issues; or 3) if we did happen to overhear our parents talk about money, our neighbors usually heard it too.

Arguments over money are cited as the number-one reason for marital discord in America. Couples need to find methods to agree on mutual and independent financial goals as well as procedures for allocating their combined resources. This alleviates possible misunderstandings and budgetary shortfalls. Achieving the desired communication skills to handle household finances is conducive to both family stability and mutual success.

Mary's Note: Talk about money calmly. Be open about your expectations with a potential spouse. Fix money problems before they start.

Understanding that all couple relationships have two types of money-manager traits is critical. Whenever you put two people in a room and analyze their money habits, one tends to be the spender (in economic terms, the person who has a higher propensity to consume), and the other is going to be more of a saver (the person with a higher propensity to save).

Even when the differentials are slight, they are there. Be honest with yourself, and know who you are and your habits.

Additionally, everyone has different ideas on why they work. Do you work hard to be able to pay the bills? Do you work hard because you are trying to retire early? Do you just want to work to stay busy? Do you want to work to change the world? Determinations of what we need versus what we want and what is required for the future are key. Disagreements over any of these can create disharmony.

Month one (the pennies-a-day method): Many couples benefit from a game called "pennies a day." Every evening, each partner writes down all expenditures for the day, down to each penny. Just for the first month, neither partner is allowed to comment or disparage the $178 spent on new dog toys or the $235 spent on golf. For the first month, there is merely observation. Having to confess to the $4 grande mocha latte and the $80-a-week-for-new-shoes habit shows individual trends that can usually be rectified by mere observation and self-discipline.

This is the month to become aware of personal monetary tendencies and teach partners not to criticize each other's expenditures. Once couples learn to honestly share what they spend money on without fear of being chastised, the road is paved for the next stage.

Month two: During the second month, the couple agrees to spend on only what they need to survive. (Yes, I do mean for the whole month.) Wants should be ignored during this period in its entirety. I try to encourage couples using this system to spend on only the absolute necessities, such as food and gas. This month is to show couples what they can save when they curtail all needless spending. (Note: There may be expenditures one partner thinks are a need and the other views as a want. These purchases should be discussed calmly and with the goal of agreeing on what is necessary and what is not.) The first two months are extremely beneficial to the road to success because they raise the level of awareness, allowing the couple to better prepare and plan their finances.

Month three: At the start of the third month, couples are generally able to look more objectively at how purchases are made, the categories those items fall into, and where they can comfortably cut back and save. Now is the time to develop categories based on the past few months and decide together how much money should go toward various categories.

Charge it: Another method is to have couples carry virtually no cash and instead put every purchase on a joint credit card. At the end of the month, go over purchases line by line, record the expenses by category, and determine what category needs more or less attention.

Find the debt: Another strategy is to gather up all of your bills, add them up, and write the total amount on the kitchen calendar. Repeat this at the end of every month to get debt reduced to zero. For many people, simply having that amount on the calendar and seeing the debt amount drop every month is a good motivator.

Set a goal: Sometimes having a goal—such as saving for a vacation or for a down payment on a house—can motivate couples to be more conscious about their spending. They can balance the desire of ritual luncheons out with friends versus the new car that constantly seems to be out of their financial reach. Once a "want" becomes a priority for both people in a relationship and they are working cooperatively toward that goal, the more likely they are to be conscious of frivolous spending.

Before you start, here are a few rules you should use when discussing money at home:

1. Be honest about expenditures. If you jointly decide that you each get $50 a week for play, write it down as a category.

2. No yelling! When the decibel level increases, the communication

efficiency decreases. So if one person gets animated, agree to postpone the discussion until both people are calm.

3. Be equal in making decisions. No, not on every little purchase, but be in agreement on how to approach money management. Having one spouse say "You do everything" doesn't count as equal.

4. Make sure each person gets "mad money"—money you can spend however you want in a set amount every month. (Calling it "mad

money" sounds more fun and less restrictive than "allowance.")

5. Learn more. Read more about finances and how to maximize resources (see next section).

Enjoy yourself: People work for money so they can enjoy life to its fullest. If you and your partner use money only as a source of argument, why bother? The income you earn should be enjoyed as much as possible. This does not mean spending it without thought to why you are spending or exactly what you are spending it on. The economic concept of scarcity is evident—we cannot satisfy all of our wants at zero costs, but many couples don't discuss what it is they *can't* afford. As a couple, you can have anything you want; you just can't have everything you want. So, set a goal and save for it.

Money is "a tool you need if you don't die tomorrow," according to the movie *Wall Street*. Regular money talks should be part of the communication that brings people closer as they achieve common goals.

A few money thoughts:

1. Money is a tool to do good things for other people.

2. Money, or the promise of money, can make some people do things they shouldn't do.

3. Money doesn't buy happiness, but poverty can be miserable.

Money $mart

$

Resources

Mary's favorite books on personal finances are:

Eric Tyson. *Let's Get Real About Our Money*. (Great for people from 16-40 years old.) Available at: http://www. amazon.com/Lets-Get-Real-About-money/dp/0132341611/ref=sr_1_1?ie=U TF8&qid=1334934628&sr=8-1

Suze Orman. *The Money Book for the Young, Fabulous, and Broke*. (Especially good on how to improve FICO scores.) Available at: http://www.amazon .com/Money-Book-Young-Fabulous-

Broke/dp/1594482241/ref=sr_1_1?s=bo
oks&ie=UTF8&qid=1334934715&sr=1-1

David Chilton's *The Wealthy Barber*
is about $10 and it is a book that I
highly recommend for all couples to
read together. It reads like a novel
and can be quickly applied. (Oldie
but a goodie—the best book for
getting couples focused on the same
financial goals.) Available at: http://
www.amazon.com/THE-WEALTHY-
BARBER-DavidChilton/dp/B000SAI072/
ref=sr_1_fkmr0_2?s=books&ie=UTF8&qi
d=1334934752&sr=1-2-fkmr0

Eric Tyson. *Personal Finance for Dummies*. Available at:http://www.amazon.com/Personal-Finance Dummies-Eric-Tyson/dp/1118117859/ref=sr_1_fkmr0_1?s=books&ie=UTF8&qid=1334934781&sr=1-1-fkmr0

Eric Tyson. *Mutual Funds for Dummies*. Available at: http://www.amazon.com/Mutual-Funds-For-Dummies-6th/dp/0470623217/ref=sr_1_1?s=books&ie=UTF8&qid=1334934811&sr=1-1

The Time Value of Money working for you

Age	Scout 1 Amount Invested		Value at 10% Return	Scout 2 Amount Invested		Value at 10% Return
22	$5,000	$5,500	$5,500	$0	$0	$0
23	$5,000	$10,500	$11,550	$0	$0	$0
24	$5,000	$16,550	$18,205	$0	$0	$0
25	$5,000	$23,205	$25,526	$0	$0	$0
26	$5,000	$30,526	$33,578	$0	$0	$0
27	$5,000	$38,578	$42,436	$0	$0	$0
28	$5,000	$47,436	$52,179	$0	$0	$0
29	$0	$52,179	$57,397	$5,000	$5,000	$5,500
30	$0	$57,397	$63,137	$5,000	$10,500	$11,550
31	$0	$63,137	$69,451	$5,000	$16,550	$18,205
32	$0	$69,451	$76,396	$5,000	$23,205	$25,526
33	$0	$76,396	$84,036	$5,000	$30,526	$33,578
34	$0	$84,036	$92,439	$5,000	$38,578	$42,436
35	$0	$92,439	$101,683	$5,000	$47,436	$52,179
36	$0	$101,683	$111,851	$5,000	$57,179	$62,897
37	$0	$111,851	$123,036	$5,000	$67,897	$74,687
38	$0	$123,036	$135,340	$5,000	$79,687	$87,656
39	$0	$135,340	$148,874	$5,000	$92,656	$101,921
40	$0	$148,874	$163,761	$5,000	$106,921	$117,614
41	$0	$163,761	$180,138	$5,000	$122,614	$134,875
42	$0	$180,138	$198,151	$5,000	$139,875	$153,862
43	$0	$198,151	$217,966	$5,000	$158,862	$174,749
44	$0	$217,966	$239,763	$5,000	$179,749	$197,724
45	$0	$239,763	$263,739	$5,000	$202,724	$222,996
46	$0	$263,739	$290,113	$5,000	$227,996	$250,795
47	$0	$290,113	$319,125	$5,000	$255,795	$281,375
48	$0	$319,125	$351,037	$5,000	$286,375	$315,012
49	$0	$351,037	$386,141	$5,000	$320,012	$352,014
50	$0	$386,141	$424,755	$5,000	$357,014	$392,715
51	$0	$424,755	$467,230	$5,000	$397,715	$437,487
52	$0	$467,230	$513,954	$5,000	$442,487	$486,735
53	$0	$513,954	$565,349	$5,000	$491,735	$540,909
54	$0	$565,349	$621,884	$5,000	$545,909	$600,500
55	$0	$621,884	$684,072	$5,000	$605,500	$666,050
56	$0	$684,072	$752,479	$5,000	$671,050	$738,155
57	$0	$752,479	$827,727	$5,000	$743,155	$817,470
58	$0	$827,727	$910,500	$5,000	$822,470	$904,717
59	$0	$910,500	$1,001,550	$5,000	$909,717	$1,000,689
	$35,000		$1,001,550	$155,000		$1,000,689

Money $mart

$

Social Capital

One thought: As you build wealth, you
also build social capital. Social capital
is how people build communities. This
happens when people form bridge clubs
and bowling leagues, hold church
bazaars, sponsor bingo at the local
school, coach Little League, take Girl
Scouts camping, help librarians read to
children, and build dog parks.

Social capital is when homeowners
band together to clean snow off their
roads, keep playgrounds in good
condition, and walk their kids to the

bus stop together. When you a buy a house, you are also buying the community where your house is located.

So, work to build a strong community. Pitch in. Volunteer. Money helps, but communities also need your time and talent. Get involved and stay involved!

I wish you financial security, great success in your community, and tremendous happiness.

Let me know how you are doing!

Let's talk about managing money on Facebook at:

www.facebook.com/groups/money smartnow

E-mail me at:
Mary@ProductiveLeaders.com

Like my Facebook page:
www.facebook.com/DrMaryKelly

Follow me on Twitter:
twitter.com/MaryKellySpeaks

Connect with me on LinkedIn:
www.linkedin.com/#/marykellytalks

Connect with me on Google Plus:
gplus.to/marykelly

Sign up for my free newsletter at:
www.ProductiveLeaders.com